Amazing
Dogs

FIRST EDITION
Series Editor Deborah Lock; **US Senior Editor** Shannon Beatty; **Project Art Editor** Hoa Luc;
Art Director Martin Wilson; **Pre-Production Producer** Dragana Puvacic;
Reading Consultant Linda Gambrell, PhD

THIS EDITION
Editorial Management by Oriel Square
Produced for DK by WonderLab Group LLC
Jennifer Emmett, Erica Green, Kate Hale, *Founders*

Editors Grace Hill Smith, Libby Romero, Michaela Weglinski;
Photography Editors Kelley Miller, Annette Kiesow, Nicole DiMella; **Managing Editor** Rachel Houghton;
Designers Project Design Company; **Researcher** Michelle Harris; **Copy Editor** Lori Merritt;
Indexer Connie Binder; **Proofreader** Larry Shea; **Reading Specialist** Dr. Jennifer Albro;
Curriculum Specialist Elaine Larson

Published in the United States by DK Publishing
1745 Broadway, 20th Floor, New York, NY 10019
Copyright © 2023 Dorling Kindersley Limited
DK, a Division of Penguin Random House LLC
22 23 24 25 26 10 9 8 7 6 5 4 3 2 1
001-333888-May/2023

A catalog record for this book
is available from the Library of Congress.
HC ISBN: 978-0-7440-7166-5
PB ISBN: 978-0-7440-7167-2

DK books are available at special discounts when purchased in bulk for sales promotions, premiums,
fundraising, or educational use. For details, contact: DK Publishing Special Markets,
1745 Broadway, 20th Floor, New York, NY 10019
SpecialSales@dk.com

Printed and bound in China

The publisher would like to thank the following for their kind permission to reproduce their images:
a=above; c=center; b=below; l=left; r=right; t=top; b/g=background
Dreamstime.com: Charles Aghoian 1, Robhainer 23, Aleksandr Zotov 6–7;
Getty Images / iStock: MirasWonderland 4–5; **Shutterstock.com:** KPG-Payless2 7cra

Cover images: *Back:* **Shutterstock.com:** Hangouts Vector Pro cra

All other images © Dorling Kindersley
For more information see: www.dkimages.com

For the curious
www.dk.com

Amazing Dogs

Laura Buller

Contents

Meeting Dogs

Dogs bark and sniff each other to say hello.

There are all kinds of dogs.
Some are very tiny.
Other dogs
are very big.
Whatever the
size, dogs can
be helpers
and heroes!

Dogs belong to an animal family called mammals. They have fur, or hair, like all mammals. You are a mammal, too!

hair

Baby dogs are called puppies. They drink milk from their mothers. Milk helps puppies grow bigger and stronger.

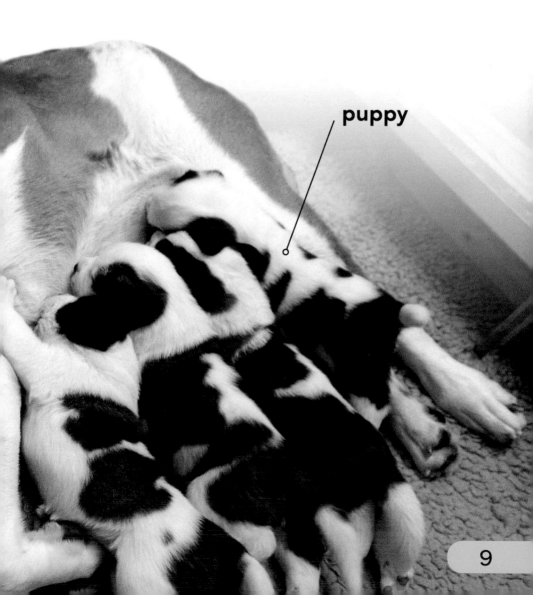

puppy

Super Senses

Dogs have super-strong senses. They can see better than you can— even in dim light.

They perk up their ears to hear sounds— even when you think it is quiet. But a dog's real superpower is its sense of smell.

nose

Sniff!

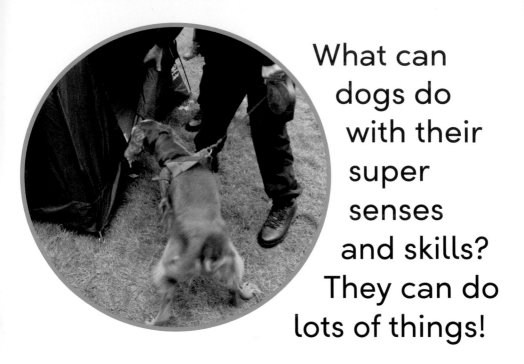

What can dogs do with their super senses and skills? They can do lots of things!

They can use their nose to pick up the scent of someone who is hurt or lost. They can also help rescue people who are trapped.

A rescue worker and a rescue dog search for people who might be trapped after a disaster.

Round Up!

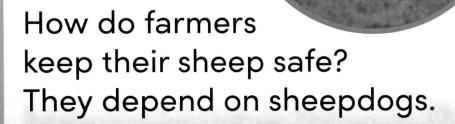

How do farmers
keep their sheep safe?
They depend on sheepdogs.

These dogs keep the sheep together and help them move in the right direction. They do this by barking and running around the sheep.

How is a herd of cattle kept together? This is the job of a smart cattle dog.

A cattle dog can help a cow if it strays from the herd. It nips the cow's ankle and the cow returns to the herd.

Nip! Nip!

A rancher and a cattle dog round up cattle.

Pooch Power!

It's freezing cold
near the snowy North Pole.

Brrrrrrr!

But this team of brave husky dogs gets the job done. They work together to pull a heavy sled.

"Mush!" cries the driver, as the dogs pull and pull.

Mush!

This mountain dog is big and strong. Farmers have used dogs like this to help with their jobs.

They would hitch the dog to a wooden cart. The cart was loaded with milk, cheese, fruit, and vegetables. The dog pulled the cart to the market.

Dogs on Duty

These dogs are not being nosy. They are using their keen sense of smell to help the police.

Sniff!

Sniff!

Police sniffer dogs do all kinds of useful work.

They can sniff out bad things and sense danger.

"Help!" Someone is in trouble. Call in the rescue dogs!

A person may get lost or stuck, or be in danger.
A rescue dog uses its sniffing skills to find the person.
Then rescue workers can get the person out of trouble.

Helping Paws

Some people need a little extra help. There are smart dogs to help!

Dogs help people who are unable to see, hear, or get around. These helpful dogs make jobs easier and safer for people.

Dogs can make people feel good. They can give emotional support to children with autism. Dogs can also cheer up people who are sick or injured. They can help people who feel lonely.

Thank you, dogs, for all the amazing things you do!

Glossary

Cattle
The name for a group of cows

Herd
A group of animals that are all the same

Mammals
A group of animals that have fur or hair, are warm-blooded, and have backbones

North Pole
The most northern place on Earth

Rescue
To save someone from a dangerous place or situation

Senses
The ways an animal explores its environment, usually through smell, seeing, hearing, taste, and touch

Sheepdog
A dog that is trained to round up sheep and keep them safe from wild animals

Sled
A small vehicle on runners used to travel over snow or ice

Index

Quiz

Answer the questions to see what you have learned. Check your answers in the key below.

1. What is a dog's best sense?

2. How do cattle dogs keep cows in the herd?

3. What does the driver of a sled say to the husky dogs?

4. How did mountain dogs help farmers?

5. What animal family do dogs belong to?

1. Its sense of smell 2. Dogs nip the cows on their ankles
3. Mush! 4. They pulled carts with heavy loads to the market
5. Dogs are mammals